Having Been an Accomplice

WINNER OF THE 2011 LEXI RUDNITSKY FIRST BOOK PRIZE IN POETRY

Laura Cronk

Having Been
an Accomplice

A Karen & Michael Braziller Book
PERSEA BOOKS / NEW YORK

Persea Books, Inc.
277 Broadway
New York, NY 10007

Library of Congress Cataloging-in-Publication Data
Cronk, Laura, 1977–
Having been an accomplice / Laura Cronk.—1st ed.
    p. cm.
Includes bibliographical references.
Poems.
ISBN 978-0-89255-413-3 (original trade pbk. : alk. paper)
I. Title.

PS3603.R664H38 2012
811'.6—dc23

                        2011042830

First edition
Printed in the United States of America
Designed by Rita Lascaro

For Megin Jimenez and for David Wilson

Contents

Having Been an Accomplice

I. Selected from the Wheel of Night

Would I Be Able to Stand

Would I be able to stand
a horse charging past?
Stand still as it approached?
The earth changing fast under its hooves,
the body slick, enormous.
I think I wouldn't flinch.

But even in thought, in quiet,
long after the horse had gone
shrinking up over the hill,
I wouldn't know you.
You, coming close
enough to graze me.

Entering

Moonscape of snow at night—
to die, to crash,

could be a crush of snow.
All softness.

I imagine, driving alone,
being enveloped by snow, crashed into, quickly.

The mice must have these visions.
Talking quietly when they can't sleep

about tunneling in endless grain until
full of it, it takes them.

Selected from the Wheel of Night

TELL ME, UNREAL,
what you thought of—
what you reeled from—
what moved you to pick up a pen?

Tell me again.
You told me
but that wasn't real.
Your feather, dipped in ink—
where did you find it, what bird?

Tell me, as your face
neared mine
where else were you?
Who else's bed?

*

This almost
opium den—
why now?
When I am old, stooped,
I expected you then.

I'm coming to—
I'm writing back—
You let me feel I was writing back.

I want to be with you
        —no—
Tell me where to find you
        —I don't know—

You're turning up again
sitting above me in a chrome chair

while I'm on the floor
with another woman.

What are you doing here?
Reminding me I'm married

and it's not even to you.
Why have you gone gray?

And why, when I saw you last,
were you resigned to such sad work?

In that dream, you had to cut the dancers
as you sculpted them.

Gray sky, gray water, cool light sand,
and pale bodies.

A rush of wind, your artist's tool,
a flash of bright warm blood.

Only now in this afterlife of dreaming
are you unveiled.

Ghosts aren't white.
They're not glowing.

They can give counsel,
just can't spend money or touch.

What we would have been alive together
is dust.

No dream, no moon
The objects are stationed
in the darkened room.

No weather, no want.
Just the bed, the stand,
the halo of an electric clock.

The ones in bed
who used to yearn or murmur
or untuck the spread

don't turn, don't nudge.
A cat outside
is leaping from a ledge.

THAT IT COULD BE THIS MOVEMENT—
tide rushing in
and dragging out—
that giving up solidity

could feel so everyday
could feel like someone
new after the undressing,
a new form to tense against
and escape from into the air—

that the leaving must feel like leaving—
a blue-lit lift and watching.
I've heard it's so and can relate.
I can conjure this almost.

WHAT THE HORSES
            drug me through,
what horses
            I hitched myself to.
Prickly scalped
            and spooked,
they rode until
            the child let loose.
Unfastened from them
            now I stand
as uninhabited
            as any man.

I HAVE MARRIED THE SUN.
His strong legs carry him
circling the neighborhood.
Glistening, he passes his hand
over the countryside.

My beloved marries me
everyday. I wait
each morning
in the dim town square,
hungry, exposed.

Later the slowness
of his heavy lidded eyes
on me,
sudden cloud cover,
hands, hot,
over and over—

His marriage to an unknown
seems not to affect
his ability to appear in public,
accept invitations,
make jokes,
unapologetic.

I am forever
strangely dressed,
baring my neck,
my middle,
my back.

I WAKE TO FIND YOU CRYING BESIDE ME.
We have been asleep
in the cabin of a flimsy boat.

We can't shake the dream you had.
Our bed is on wheels and rolls loudly
around the cabin.

It is the time of my traveling.
There has been a rocky shore,
a warm sea, stones tipping as we walk on them.

You are my companion, my guide
whose voice I can't remember.

The place we haven't been yet, our home,
you wait for me there.

I know you keep your money in a drawer.
We present ourselves
dripping from the shower.

We give and accept praise.
I don't remember what you say, I just remember
loving your face as you speak and your voice.

I know we have concurrent dreams.

I travel but I don't write it down.
That is another woman.
I don't have anything to give you.

This is the year I dream I have a fine view
from a second story room,
a huge, clean window in wooden casing.

Or is that a place I go alone?
Do I dream any of this at all?

A woman comes up and blocks the view.
The light, the scene, everything changes,
everything that I can see around her.

I DIDN'T LOVE YOU.
I didn't see you.
I saw you for a moment,
a shadow.

There was that dinner party,
but I didn't meet you.
God loves death
just as much as birth,

and who knows
how much that is.
Your inner life,
—*I didn't know you*—

connected to mine.
The point of it, Bitter Wit,
is to rid me, Inner Life,
of tenderness toward you.

Cockleburr, Milkweed.
Lambsquarter, Wild Carrot Seed,
no place for them
and they grow.

BEING IN LOVE MAKES
it hard to communicate
with anyone in any way at all.

It means walking into the lake
with you
over and over.

This feeling of sinking.
I can say this. You know it too.
We're in love.

Here we go, down we go,
the unsayable
between us, we accept it.

I awoke in the middle.
Apple trees were rooted visibly,
rotting apples and new ones
amid exposed, numerous roots.

The smell of rotten apples and new ones
was heavy and sweet or light and sweet
depending on the wind.

Though I knew
the farmer could appear,
I knew, along with this,
that I was quite alone.

Birds clamored
in the way of birds
listening to other birds,
with nothing lurking.

My mother said instantly,
though I thought I was alone,
Always pretend you're a tiny animal.
You are prey.

You should be alert
in the natural way
when you are alone.

I considered her and went half back
to being myself—
my legs beginning to chill,

my back against the knotted trunk,
the sky holding onto its blue
in the late afternoon—

But I'm not ready, I'd like to have flowers
in the room. I'd like to find something
to wear that is loose and pretty.
I wanted people around.

I don't have it worked out yet.
I wanted decorations, wax birds
hung in a circle. I wanted to make sure
somehow there would be a breeze.

I'm not ready. Everything I've been,
a bird, a dog in a field, a wire
hung from the house to a post,
a can of cold beer in the garage,
a girl on a motor bike, a little boy
in love, I thought I would have them all
with me. I can't worry now, I just have to go.

You say it's coming. You say it
and a lake tumbles out onto the floor
I slip getting to the room. I know
where to go to wash and prepare.

From the Other

What is small is smaller, suddenly.
Her shoulder, small, with my hand on it,
her ferociousness is something I can grip.
I am so hungry for anything. Blind.

My blindness finds its course, surging.
She is what I am surging
towards, through, pushing in makes her
fragment, disperse, hover.

The resistance her body makes,
it is the resistance
air makes for a wounded flyer.
Won't she take me in farther?

Horse Neck-deep in Water

Horse neck-deep in water. There's a moving through and moving through. The full strong breast of the horse is morning and day. Its thin legs and mane are night. It walked all day and night through the water and won't last much longer. I confessed my love, confessed all my debt, last night. The night before I wore an older kind of undergarment. Thick ribbons holding up stockings, wire and firm mesh. I knew I would be climbing into the river and this would be what to wear. Black bridle. I wore these things and washed my face, took down my hair, slipped down the wet grass, left my things on the bank, left streaks in the mud and climbed into the water. Or I wish I had. I'll think of it again, slipping on the wet grass and mud, entering the water, my place of entry easily seen, marks of my heels sliding in the mud. The bottom of the river was slick with muck, the river had an imperceptible current, or no, actually I wanted the bottom to be slick, but there was a current and the bottom was sharp with rocks. I think of the horse, dream horse, painted horse, totem horse, solitary horse unknown to others, glimpsed in sleep. I watch the beginning of its movement, the limbs learning to move in the black water, and find myself what I was before any of this, before it became very late and the river became black. In the blackness, with the turtles climbing in and out along the sides of the river, I am what I was before and will continue to be. I am a fat little sparrow. Incapable of entering. I watch all night. In the morning I sing about the river and what I saw climbing in. My song sounds cheerful, as it always does. There's nothing I can do to change the sound.

I Have Humbled Myself beneath the Night Sky

I have humbled myself beneath the night sky and beneath the sky of early morning. I have walked a long way tied into a wool coat, the belt cutting my waist (lie). I have walked a long way with the sun heavy and hot upon me. I have walked penance (lie), run penance (lie), worked slowly at a desk toward penance (big lie), chopped vegetables for stew in penance. I have lain down on the bare earth (lie), on the bare floor (lie). I have waited in penance on the stairwell (lie). Though I didn't know that every movement of my body was penance (many lies), my mind, waking and in sleep, was committing acts of penance. Though penance cannot be paid, it must be paid. Though you benefit in no way from my penance, walking in the imaginary field, shivering, in the dark, does open a sliver of the night sky through which I glimpse you.

Back when We Hadn't Done Anything We Wouldn't Do Again

Back when we didn't have to say anything but yes. Do you want to meet up—yes. And take a walk—yes. Do you want to walk through Chinatown—yes. And over the Brooklyn Bridge—yes. Do you want to get something to eat—yes. Maybe tacos and a little pitcher of sangria—yes. Do you want to walk me home—yes. And will you now please not leave—yes. Do you want to run away together—yes. And hike on snowy hilltops—yes. Even though we're unprepared, no gloves—yes. Would you like to sit and read together—yes. For a very long time—yes. Do you want to take a shower—yes. While I wait sipping whiskey in a slip—yes. Would you like to get married—yes. Outside—yes. On a beautiful day—yes. Surrounded by soft green bean fields—yes. With the violin player, a friend, missing notes—yes. With a minister we found on the internet—yes. With our families smiling at us—yes. With warm sun—yes. With a breeze—yes. In love, with radiant faces—yes, yes.

You Come for Fear

You come for fear of the other men,
the ones who wait at the port
for the ship to dock.

You know they want
a sea captain. You know
that my waist is still supple,

my legs still strong.
You know how much money
I send home but you know

how much the men at the port
waiting there leaning on the ropes
think a captain has when she returns.

I'll come home,
walk down the unsteady board
to you, the wind on your face,

your hair freshly washed.
Smelling not of salt and yeast,
the thick smells of the ship
and its women.

Smelling like earth,
peppery and warm,
you'll wear your good jacket.

We'll walk together
home to the stew you've made,
to the house carefully arranged,

the fiddle in the corner. I'll wait for you to play;
I won't ask. I'll start to clean up.
You'll take the fiddle to the back.

You'll play, the fiddle so small
in your hands, face bent over it, eyes closed.
You'll play the ancient song

that makes a woman's legs grow land-bound
and unable to go to sea.
The rite that rarely works but could.

You'll play, your large hands, one black nail,
one blood blister, the calluses and notches
in your finger tips, the song too long,

too hopeful and strange, too much
in it of what we know is wrong,
sinful even to ask for.

I don't want to be at the prow of a ship.
I don't want the women waiting
for their orders. I don't want the gasping

deaths of the fish dumped out on the deck.
I want the pagan love song
my husband plays to keep me here.

Darling, You Are the World's Fresh Ornament

Darling, you are the world's fresh ornament.
Ne'er a bigger bloom could a seeker find
Than this that you, dear fool, have on displayment.
The displacement of my gentle mind
To boudoir regions, gaudy cunning luxury,
Has my old self-substantial petrol in short supply.
To run this rearing gal, the new polished buxomry
Demands a man—the night's auto reply
To teenish hungers doesn't cut it.
Give me tender pullings of the world one way
And another, and I'll give right back.
That's the way to increase, to fight the lack.

New American Forest

This is the new American forest.
You seduce me with the food you gather,
I seduce you with the food I gather.
We don't waste. What we are building
benefits from each choice piece
as well as from each salvageable piece.

We've come here through the groves
of hemlock dying with pests.
We walk through the standing dead into living trees,
through the forest and farther until we reach the stream.
We follow as it gathers. We walk to the falls.

We were mad to be in contact with each other.
Now we are in contact with each other.
We are in contact with branches and leaves,
air, sun, with the darkness at night.

As we walk the narrowing trails,
pushing back thorny branches,
everything becomes denser, darker, more in the middle,
less beginning, less end, more lost clung together,
more rising on wobbly legs.

We slept in the open at first,
now we make a place for ourselves where we go.
I know that I could swell with you, but
you could also swell with me.
Look, we've actually become thinner together,
taking what we need, saving even more.

Break that Knot Again

Disarmed, I am battered
      by a three-person'd god,
banished into the sacrament

of a new body, a hut on a pond,
      the trinity of my body and yours has done it.
My body, yours, and something else.

Tell me,
      please, how this hut
was built.

Was it built in a frenzy
      of male and female effort?

Effort, that protestant word.

      *

You happened to take the shape
      so perfectly of a man
that I couldn't help but be lost in my distraction.

My distraction took on spiritual proportions.
      I'll say again, again, the world is going to hell
in the cheapest plastic hand basket

but I'm moving farther and farther
	away from that world. I was, I am moving toward your lips,
I'm moving toward you—

You, who persuade me to forget
	what I rid myself of—
what we—

Though you shut the door on it,
	though I have locked myself in rooms with it,
Look! I'm ensnared again with life.

Mutinied, ferried,
	enthralled, accompanied
by one who will look like you, who will look like me.

	*

I had been pent up in rooms high in towers
	paying penance, trying to communicate
an impossible narrative to an impossible recipient.

But then I shed my long skirts, my cape, my boots
	laced to the knee, my layers of underthings.
I shed my rings and bracelets, my embroidered stripes and chevrons.

Beadless, unadorned, simple, without shoes, in the absence
	Of a believeable god, I traded it all
for a shift—

I found the hut we had abandoned.
　　　I entered
and the building was finished in a night.

I fished in the pond there and made small fires. It was the air
　　　in the trees that set me with child.
I did my work slowly and found myself remade.

　　　　　*

Now when I return,
　　　eyes flashing, hair full, face flushed,
it is that I am coming back to the world.

　　Not to the world I was fighting, but to you,

full of moon and sun. What is unweak, true.
　　　The paintings of the Spanish cathedrals are alive
under my skin, the peonies of summer hang heavy when I wake,

the man, earth-made man, strong as the many horses in the field,
　　　tender as the newly knitted bone, supple in half-dream lies quiet
when I, disarmed, go down to sleep.

Having Been

She just wanted
To keep eating strawberries
And drinking diet rite
Wanted to keep eating tomatoes
And riding her bike
Whatever it was
Quadrupling inside
Was also going
With her to the store
In the rain
To buy bleach
She called to say
I'm running away
With our baby
It was a joke
She wouldn't
Any of it
Except a surgeon
With a tan and a mask
Monk's garb at the end
Of a tunnel of bright white light
The overhead lights of an ethereal office
A photographer's blasting white
Amplified lights
The process of dying
As a practice
As something to practice
Before work, after,
On weekends
So young
There was clover stuck
In her hair
She picked it out
To go to work.

*

Young, he built something
Around himself
That said on all sides
Husband
Dreamt himself a fish
Had to wake
To go to work
To fund among other things
A birthday party
Celebrating not being so young
Anymore birthday party
With the grief
Of the next day
Under their coats
She didn't have a drink
At the party
Had the best sparkling
Water ever bottled
Hoping not to but hoping to
Why and wherefore
Wherever young couples
Go early on Saturday mornings
They leave those places in cabs
Gray faced—but it could have been the rain—
The cab driver driving them,
Any two people tethered together,
Bound together in grave March weather.

II. Having Been an Accomplice

The President's Companion

While I was a young woman with my hair long and tied back, I walked outside, lost in thought, scuffing my boots. You spoke from your post through the speakers and the televisions, and when you paused to take a breath, you heard the sounds of a young woman walking. Two people unknown to each other.

Soon I took notice of the armed guards in the subway and looked closely at these extensions of you. Called to, I kept walking, disappearing into the river of passengers leaving the station.

And then I stopped walking. I sat in contemplation and the signs of your attention poured over me. I had been your counterpoint all along and I chose to join you in your gardens and rooms.

That we found ourselves together in the ritual of the everyday, in the ritual of opening the notebook and writing, the ritual of consulting the newspaper, the ritual of standing before the questioning crowds, does not speak to my ingenuity but to the way of the world forever.

Your back slumped as you sat at your desk preparing to leave this office. I, older now, will meet you on the other side. Everything I have learned about consequence, I've learned from you.

Having Been an Accomplice

I CLIMB THE TOWER STAIRS. MY BREATH PUFFS HOT IN THE AIR.
    Coming upon a small
cut window in the spiral, I look out to an icicled world, coldness
    arched over everything.

The skirts I've worn outside drag heavy up the tight passageway
    collecting
frozen dust, the wool damp and darkening.

I could have taken the elevator, but no, not when I have the royal
    feeling burning—I've been reading the paper again—not when
    I'm ready to see something and respond.

Like the others, this is a fake feeling. I reach my door and need a key
    for the lock.

My apartment is #21. The super has slipped a note under the door
    which I step over.
I go straight for the back in search of my best, my most sumptuous,
    most well-fitted clothes.

I went straight for the back, but now I'm pacing, pacing. I'll never
    read the paper again.

From my window I see boys in big coats, they're signing up on the
    drafty sidewalk, signing clipboards. In a flash, I see it, what's
    happening so far away and it seizes me. What was I thinking? It
    could have been avoided. I should have spoken sooner.

I wear the brooch that makes me a general. I sit in the deepest
    chamber of my apartment dressed to kill and issue orders. But
    I send them out and get nothing back. Send them out and get
    nothing back.

I SAT IN THE DEEPEST CHAMBER OF MY APARTMENT DRESSED TO
kill and issued orders. But I sent them out and got nothing back.

That I thought the king was mine: madness. That I thought I could
stop him if only I conjured the right thought. Like praying, I
thought that what I did inside meant something.

I could say, "Back when I wasn't the boss I was in a much less good
mood" and "everything follows on the spangled light of that."

It's true that I used to be in a much worse mood. It's true that the lighting has improved. Here's to that.

Parties are mine to throw, they're mine, no matter who's coming. I have my influence, my ruling class, my own personal celebrity.

I've tried the other way. But wearing a kerchief wasn't doing any
    good. Taking recipes
from the people for chicken with cream of chicken soup—

I don't want to make that kind of thing. I don't want to address it.

Better to stop the war by doing my hair. Coaxing out amazing lift,
    peaceful waves,
light catching waft.

Going to the War Resisters' League tonight wouldn't have done any
    good anyway. Their protest song calendar didn't get one arrow
    through the armored beast. Lest we forget, the thing is covered
    in armor and is a beast.

We'll have roast tarragon chicken and the freshest best asparagus
    and pastes on toasts.
I'm dreaming. There is no we.

Just they. I see them all in a flash out commiserating in the yard in
    the dark. The troops I call them when they betray me like this.
    You tell the troops to do things, and when they do them, you
    punish them.

But not now. Now is the time for dinner. I pull the dead chicken out
of the plastic.
The chicken's been through hell and back. Or, though it was living,
it's not organic.

Out of timelessness and into this.

Not Defeatist. More Artist.

Not Leftist. More Painless. More hidden, more lawless. By that I
mean I have no law degree. I'm a woman cooking. Not hopeless.
Well, now that I look at it.

I CAME UPON A MASS GRAVE UNCOVERED.
The bodies after years had turned to pound-sized stones,

or jewels, smooth as glass and heavy.
They were puckered on either end like mouths.

This was what happened to the ones who suffered,
who had been saints and were killed.

The governing body doesn't love
the small parts of its body.

Looking my own sadism in the mirror.
The government I run. A little being

chewed its own feet off and died in agony,
the chemicals of escape used up.

Putting a screaming being into a plastic bag:
my governance. Trash barrels, when upended,

dump small, weighty stones. I should forfeit my standing.
I still go on picnics with people who kid around.

Who fool each other with basketballs,
trip each other up. I lied, I'm not all grass

and honey for you. A woman waiting under a lonely tree,
fresh from the solitude of that.

I should be ready to sit at the massive table,
share the evening, begin a fair kingdom, private.

I should prepare to load my bags
to visit the dying and the dead.

But it's late and I've become for sure
cruel out of laziness.

I eat everything I want. All that I've seen
consumed and gone.

I eat delicacies that are deaths
of poor, soft things. I eat them up.

I ALWAYS KNOW WHEN THERE'S BEEN AN UNINVITED GUEST,
                    when we've been infiltrated.

Before even opening the door I sense the pest,
                    my whole mood adulterated.

We must ask him back! I've got something boiling on the stove. Potatoes
                    glop up to the surface, fish heads.

Let me get my ruffled apron with the pallid paisley, my
                    hired hand,

my steel spoons with their skull insignias, my little
                    hunchback way of getting the door.

Darling, would you fix our guest another drink—cracked glass,
                    split lip, salted rim.

Hostess cheeks have been pinched. Linoleum has been waxed.
                    What was frizzy,

greasy, stacked and cinched, now hidden in low light
                    and a blast of Pledge.

Don't mind the crackling of tiny feet along the walls,
                    the black boxes,

the silver platter with the wooden stake, the crucifix
                    hovering over the sideboard.

Coming in through the window? Looking for some electronica,
                    a gold watch

A powdered donut to make your mouth
                            look dead?

Stay. We'd love to have your head.

WHAT DEATH IS
>for one thing
>>is not enough food

I am not dead
>I am dressed for dinner
>>how Eva Braun

to be in this dress
>bright and floral
>>to be wearing this

turquoise necklace
>to have smoothed hair
>>and coral lips

like her I've wanted
>beautiful moments unlike her
>>I hunch over my plate

the legions of dead
>offer us their food
>>these aren't vegetarian meals

this isn't aesthetic eating
>if I wasn't so hungry
>>I could dish out seconds for him

pass over half of my dessert
>with his mouth full of something sweet
>>I could have some sway

but my greed is unified
      with his greed—the table is full—
         I say nothing and we eat.

I WAKE ON THE TRAIN TO FIND
Blood drenching my shirt.

I don't want it,
I ask not to receive it,

That which is given to me.
The forces on the ground

The rhetoric in headphones
All around. Compulsively, I rule

What falls to my jurisdiction.
I nodded off feeling ill

And wake dying —
I had given up praying, meditative

Walking, reading, dreaming.
I was given

The abandoned man
And his stench on the church steps.

Traveling among headlines
I don't have my wallet, forgot it,

No keys and no phone
But somehow I have access

to a direct line
That runs to whatever it is

That decides.
Voices gurgling, pleading, bubbling

Along the line.
I'll pick it up just this time.

I STOOD ON A STAGE IN A DARK CABARET AND SPOKE CLEARLY about what needed to happen. Journalists took note. Springtime, commanded to commence, commenced. Suffering, commanded to stop, stopped. Power changed hands, changed hands, kept changing, became a sound, sounds. I walked right out of the front door, past all of them scribbling, took my path to cross the river.

"oh what a multitude / of springtimes / have been packed into my feverish body"

I paraded over the bridge like a brown bear, like a Mayakovski, full of natural force, a surge of a flood, that's how I walked. Not a contradictory thought, like a headstrong bird slowed by a fat breast, like a great dane—huge, head up, strong loping walk; a flamenco dancer walking, my clothes commanded to swish. From one end of the bridge to the other I walked, a show for anyone who might see— *now that's someone spitfire, sure, split of lightning, ramrod, shining axe, glistening steely tale of comet, a streak, a parade of one.*

MIDWAY. I'M FROZEN IN THE MIDDLE. Suspended, looking at the water.

There's smog on either side of the bridge, pollution shimmering. On one side are the Centers for Peace Studies, their Research Programs. On the other side are the grocery stores. I do want groceries.

I want to stop the war, but I've been consumed with so many things. All of the small actions that go into this. All of the preparing food and eating it. All of the dressing and undressing. Not just showering, but singing in the shower. Laundry.

Small actions in direct opposition to the thoughts of the Research Centers. This cooking and then eating dinner in front of the TV. Not watching satire, watching a singing competition.

I want to walk deeply into the darkness, nude as a god, through the self into the darkness.

I want to blow up the Law with Language, having run my tongue around my mouth ten thousand times. Instead of not speaking, I want to speak.

MY RULE AND MY REACH WILL COLLAPSE
into a shadow of hair.

Collapse further into a stain
on the floor.

Body, so watery and delicate.
living on air and prepared dishes.

This smallness frets me,
no I fret it. I am laced in tight to it.

Breathlessness. Throats
I slit or would have slit

to prevent my own slitting,
to remain for even a moment more.

The police will descend and ascend,
moving up and down the ladder of heaven.

When I look at them to join them
I will be spitting.

I will be as horrid as anything dying,
as unapproachable, my ladylike nature

intact, not tacked on, but in
and spilling out.

My governance,
my jurisdiction is tainted

With cowardliness, with what I've done
for my own advance.

The revolutionaries stack themselves
as wood and burn.

Then stack themselves again and burn.
Their demand is fair: my end.

But I can't. I've a very small time
left in the palace.

I've got to go out on the balcony again
and feel the air.

A Citizen Queen

Parading around, pomp, pomp, pomp,
      red bulbs on a chain around my neck.
Powdered collarbones to be shown off
      with a swish and stomp, pomp, pomp, pomp,
skirts tight in the back for the queenly pomp.

*

Stomping around my apartment, stomp, stomp, stomp.
The mice don't even know it's me that's killing them.
Ha! They think it's all bad luck,
Ha! I'm here and I've got teeth and claws—

Queenly pearls and pomp, pearly voice,
I've got the queenly feeling welling up. I'm bursting with
a vitality of the flesh, flesh singing in a key that makes
subordinate other flesh. Subordinate yet drawn.

The mice are stirring, perhaps it's the song I've been singing
as a folksy after-thought. Perhaps it's my perfume.
A woman like the rest they think.
This parade is just a show, they think,

But no! Stomp, stomp, pomp! Stomp, stomp, pomp!
Mousies one and mousies two, away with you, away with you.
Prepare to writhe in glue, so horrid I won't look at you.

*

Asleep on my queenly hair, I have these visions:
spiraling stairs, rooms stacked upon rooms.
In the rooms I see people sleeping.
In one, I see the executioner, and he's awake.

The sleep from the others is seeping into his room.
Surrounded by tender people,
open and tender in sleep, so tender they could be eaten
in one mouthful, this feeling is washing over him.

And he's quiet. I'm taking note. Look, he's open to something.
He's quiet and awake, he's not advancing,
He's not even thinking of his planes, maybe he's not so bad.
His blades are crossed over his legs.

*

Alone in the house, slump, slump, slump.
A life should be the movement in and out of sleep.
Why can't I sleep? No mice are squirming in their traps.
The swords and knives have been cleaned,
The house is bloodless and dry, but still I can't sleep.

An old black iron, rusted and lumpy, I'll put it on the gas stove.
Blue flames creating a solid heat. I'll wrap it in a towel
and bring it to bed. I'll come back to being just a woman.
I want to bring the strange cold dreams
while my feet fumble with a warmth that's almost living.

To cut this out and be clear, I want to set the fire myself.
But the gang with the torches would only laugh
if I came running out of the house with my clothes burning, firing a gun.
If there's going to be a fire, they'll set it.
The ones with the torches are the ones with the bombs.

*

I'm sleeping with them. I'll make them all into one:
I'm sleeping with him. Giving birth to his child,
combing his hair, feeding him, singing to him,
hoping to calm his nerves, glad that he's been gentle,

glad that he's overlooked some things.
I've been leaving out books about health,
the ones I've read. It's slow work. I kiss his face
all over. I buy meat whole and cut it apart.

I'm trying to be something from the inside, but
this discomfort makes it hard to think sometimes or read.
To cut this out and be clear, when I said *he*, I meant *they*.
When I said *me*, I meant *us*.

We're eating too much to be attractive. I'll throw up
from using their language. Where's my queenly quality
with my separate apartment? I want to say

we're all the ugly feminine,
our faces painted on . . .

Tick, tick, tick, time running out ahead.
          Looking for a subject, no subject is around.
The big round bottom slumps in its dress
          even though I'm nothing, I'm a Queen nonetheless.
A Queen as the planes go flying overhead.

Having at Least Dressed Appropriately

I want to forge the self with the darkness, with the dead, with the language that cracks out of study.

Dressing for it is the starting place, backstage cinching up into heavy gowns and a commanding coat. When I'm acting commander, I move slowly, but with force.

A fleet is waiting, with faces upturned. The decision I made hasn't crossed my lips, it's humming in my head, my throat is dry.

I said I wanted to forge the self with the darkness, but that must have been a century ago. How could I say such a thing?

I've come out onto the stage, the balcony, the pulpit. The body actually needs light, the brain needs light, study yes, but even more, brightness, light.

I tell the troops what they're going to have to do. I shiver with dread during the time it takes to marshal them down the hallway, into the very small room where the removal is to take place. It is a preservation of the self and a perversion of all else and dressed appropriately or not I can't speak well of it.

In any kind of aftermath, the body needs to dream. Mine does. Those do. We dream together. I dream with those I've made complicit with me.

Having Dreamt Complicit Dreams

When God spoke to me, I didn't hear it, though it was a sensation. My hands were tying the sash of a girl's dress when I felt the reverberations of God's voice.

I also felt God's voice in the parking lot when the homeless man confronted me. The doctor had run away, finding me needy, too forward. But the homeless man in the clinic's parking lot, though terrifying, was needful of me.

If God could be the serpent in the garden, then it is possible that God could speak to me. If God is the opposite of the serpent, but able to act as the serpent, there is a chance that I've experienced the sensation of God speaking to me.

I've been handed a child, beautiful, shining blonde, with sunlight streaming all over us. When the child spoke, she said, only, *hello*. Several times I've fed a baby at my breast, but only at one breast. The other has no milk.

And the night right after, that night I was chased. The man had a gun. I ran and ran. I found a compartment in a wall to hide in. Curled there, I waited, in horror of what was about to happen. I don't know if any of the sensations were, but was that the sensation of God speaking to me?

The Bride Queen

It worked; the empires
        have merged. I can't see out of my old eyes at all.
Surveying now with new eyes
        the rolling hills we own,
the calves being slaughtered in the distance.

The contract we made in the air holds. The contract, the promise,
the contract made in the sun, in the air, in the breeze, it holds.

        I've taken a husband.   My single ruler days through.
                His great big body gives me weak knees,   weak voice.
                        What do I mean?   What do I mean?
                Satisfaction comes   at this price.

        I'm a hivey queen, all
                blotchy and red.   The king is gone
            and I'm circling the house, claiming it
        mine,
                trying to see everything while he's out.

I stamp my foot at the loss of vision!   I'm seeing red!
My new sight is a sharpened sight but I used to be able
        to see such strange things!

Or they saw me, weird and lording about
the solitude of an apartment.   Whatever monasticism I could fake
        drew forth terrible bulls bowling through halls,
old women flying down halls. Trembling, I would follow,
heading underground toward the endless rooms.

And sometimes,   in the quiet,
        the snow fell and I saw it
exactly as it was and was   alone in it.

Before, too, I could see the whole world
and make pronouncements.

Now I'm starting to have a more provincial sight.
          Married woman queen,   bride queen,
queen of two lands that must be managed, the
rest can go to hell.

Queen in a kimono, queen scrubbing the tub, queen of a shopping cart
          haughtily choosing what to buy, queen of an erotic little family,
queen of scattered underthings, queen of the hairs on the floor,
          queen of a plate of chops, queen of deux, two, two.

The kingdom slips, oh well.
          People will carry on, one being cruel to the next.

Queen of this, just this.

          I see myself.   I'm looking at myself.
          I had been reading the reports, I can see a lot from my window,
          but I've only got an hour so I've turned to the mirror instead.

I'm blotchy and red,
          I'm all hivey and red,
unsettled and hivey and red.

Maybe that's the trouble with being queen of an apartment.
          You think you're queen of things you're not.
The vote I cast withered and died in the box.

But there are things I could do. What a nasty queen I am.
I've read the reports, I see all the fakery and I let it go unpunished.
          What a foul, selfish queen.

Because the king's on my mind with his hard kingly chest.
They're blowing up the East and I think just of our bed.

> (If you could, if you would, dear
> king, do the thing that you do, the
> caress and the flick, the very loving
> tricks you employ. If you could if you
> would so will I.)

Is that tromp outside the door his tromp? Is that him tromping up
    the steps?
        Tromp, tromp, tromp? Is that my king? Tromp, tromp, tromp.
        (My kingdom around that sound.)

These hives tell my secrets!
        I've yet to make up!
                My hair wants its pile, my neck its fat beads.
My face wants its paint. I need time to make up.
        I have layers and layers of fashionable layers
                I was going to use to make myself up.

To stomp around the apartment with all my flair and swish and pomp
        while the rooms were mine To call forth my subjects
                and let them be mine.

But no, wait,
        if it's him,
                if that tromp is his tromp,
                        it's okay I'll be fine.

Oh, I do want him of course, there go my knees.
(Wait, no, knees, stand please!)

There was something more I was going to do.
I need just a few minutes.
There was something I was ready to see.

There was a vision that ran along the wall the way a mouse
runs along the wall. As a haunt, as a psychic fear.
There were flashes of gray telling me something.

Having Walked Back and Forth Across the Bridge between my Job and my Apartment, Returning Always to a Desk

When I sat behind a powerful desk, a child climbed out from under it.

I sit at a secretary's desk. I live in an apartment. I am childless.

I rule the country. The war is my doing. I'm considering ending it. I protect my own child, but not necessarily the children of others.

Having Dreamt Archaic Dreams

Pillaging the sensitive, prying riches from their hands,
their hands with sensitive fingers, their fingers with sensitive pads,

the tips the shapes of drops,
each one dripping gold.

Children upon children hidden in the halls,
half-queens running fast to save them,

killers running fast to kill them,
half-princes worth their weight in gold.

Rubbed with salt and pummeled, kneaded and scraped and caressed,
the dead sloughed off the surface, cleansed and warm and decadent,

the victors lift their vibrant eyes, their bodies steamed and purified,
rising from forgotten baths braceleted with spoils.

The victors lift their eyes to see the proof of what they've done—
hunks of jewels stuck into gold, hammered sheets and panels of gold,

pale women carrying bowls of sweet milk on their heads,
around their ankles, gold.

Years, thousands of them, hidden behind marble walls—
mosaics of human forms, human forms in bright red robes,

halos upon halos,
the halos lit with gold.

Having Been in the Arms of the President

Though he didn't bring back
the most delicate ingredients,
I did cook well
with what he brought.

The days are getting longer,
they say the worst is over,
we'll have more light
from here on out.

Though he fought
there were no marks on his body,
there were none on mine.

The fields are burning,
but he didn't smell of smoke.
I couldn't see the smoke
in the distance.

Having Been Unprepared

He died. He died. The Voice of Voices came to me "There shall be no sign."

His death has been taken from my body, the anesthesia, cold, running into my arm. Climbing into a cab, his death has bled through my clothes.

His death has visited me as I sat with a cup of tea in my bed, the bed clothes asking to be washed. Stirring lovely, golden onions in the kitchen, his death has knocked the spoon from my hand.

His death has been my attention on the bowl of soup before me. Reading is halting, as his death calls to me from the next room.

His death has broken the routine of my bathing, my grooming. In the stainless steel basin of the sink, his death lies throbbing.

I am sitting at the window and his death is whitening the glass. I turn to work and his death has taken my chair. A suit of clothes, (my vestments, my royal garments!) lies draped there. I know now I won't wear these clothes again.

Notes

The phrase "the wheel of night" is from the Mary Jo Bang poem "T Equals Time to be Tamed" from *The Bride of E*.

"I have married the sun" is after Vladimir Mayakovsky's poem "Me."

"Back When We Hadn't Done Anything We Wouldn't Do Again" owes a debt to David Lehman's book *The Daily Mirror*.

"Darling You Are the World's Fresh Ornament" is after William Shakespeare's *Sonnet 1*.

"New American Forest" owes a debt to Walt Whitman's *Leaves of Grass*.

"Break that Knot Again" owes a debt to John Donne's "Batter my heart, three-person'd God."

"The President's Companion: A Letter" is after Ezra Pound's translation of "The River Merchant's Wife: A Letter" with some images taken from Oliver Stone's movie *W* and the final line taken from Fanny Howe's memoir *Winter Sun*.

"I came upon a mass grave" owes a debt to the Robert Bresson movie *Au hazard Balthazar*.

"What death is" owes a debt to the Oliver Hirschbiegel movie *Downfall*.

The quoted text in "Having Paraded Over the Bridge" comes from Vladimir Mayakovsky's poem "Adults" as it appears in *The Bedbug and Selected Poetry*, edited by Patricia Blake and translated by Max Hayward and George Reavey.

"I stood on a stage in a dark cabaret" owes a debt to the Helene Cixous and Catherine Clement book *The Newly Born Woman*, translated by Betsy Wing.

"Having Been Unprepared" pulls the text "There shall be no sign" from *The King James Version of the Bible*, Mark 8:10–13.

Acknowledgments

Thank you to the editors of the following publications where many of these poems first appeared, sometimes in different forms: *Barrow Street, Bat City Review, Conduit, Ecotone, H.O.W. Journal, Lyric Poetry Review, The Melic Review, No Tell Motel, RealPoetik,* and *WSQ.* Thank you also to the editors of these anthologies: *The Best American Poetry* (2006 and 2008 editions), *The Best American Erotic Poems,* and *The Bedside Guide to No Tell Motel.*

I am deeply grateful to these mentors: David Lehman, Fanny Howe, Mildred Dunaway, Catherine Bowman, Gerry Alpert, Deborah Landau and Robert Polito. Thank you to these dear and steadfast writing friends: Lori Lynn Turner, Luis Jaramillo, Leah Iannone, Lisa Freedman, Craig Morgan Teicher, Nicole Steinberg, Michael Quattrone, Penelope Cray, Joydeep Sengupta, Wende Crow, Jennifer Huh, Sean Singer, and Matthew Yeager. Thank you to my parents Patricia Cronk and Vince Cronk. Thank you to the editors of *The Vidalia Onion Society.* Thank you to my editor Gabriel Fried for his patience and vision, and heartfelt thanks to everyone at Persea Books.

Thank you most of all to Megin Jimenez, poet, friend, and sister in the cause, to Honor Moore for her support and glorious example, and to David Wilson, with much love.

About the Author

Laura Cronk has curated the Monday Night Poetry Series at KGB Bar in the East Village for many years. Her poems have appeared in numerous journals, as well as in several editions of *The Best American Poetry* series. She is Associate Director of the Writing Program at The New School University, where she coordinates the Riggio Honors Program: Writing and Democracy. Originally from New Castle, Indiana, she currently lives with her family in Jersey City.